From Rain:
Poems, 1970-2010

Also by Bruce Guernsey

New England Primer (Cherry Grove Collections, 2008)

The Lost Brigade (Water Press and Media, 2005)

Soldier's Home (Water Press and Media, 2003), limited edition

A Thousand Words (Small Poetry Press, 1998), chapbook

Peripheral Vision (Small Poetry Press, 1997), chapbook

The Invention of the Telephone (Stormline Press, 1987), chapbook

January Thaw (University of Pittsburgh Press, 1982)

Canoe/The Nest/The Apple (Ives Street Press, 1982), chapbook

Genesis (Puddingstone Press, 1975), chapbook

Lost Wealth (Basilisk Press, 1974)

Biological Clock (Katahdin Poetry Series, 1973), chapbook

Hour of the Wolf (Penyeach Press, 1972), chapbook

Shelled Flesh (Back Door Press, 1970), chapbook

For Sarah,
with an "h"

Burd

From Rain:
Poems, 1970-2010

Bruce

BRUCE GUERNSEY

ECCO QUA PRESS
Beverly, Massachusetts

FROM RAIN: POEMS, 1970 - 2010 Copyright© 2012 Bruce Guernsey.
All rights reserved. Printed in the United States of America. Cover
design by Victoria Woollen-Danner. For information address Ecco
Qua Press, 54 Lothrop Street, Beverly, Massachusetts 01915.

Library of Congress Cataloging-in-Publication Data

Guernsey, Bruce.
From Rain: Poems, 1970 - 2010 / Bruce Guernsey.— 1st. ed.
ISBN: 978-1-4675-0065-4

For my children, Brendan and Megan,
from whom I learned where words begin,

and for my dear wife Victoria,
who gave them their meaning.

CONTENTS

Part Three

Part Four

"it went as it came and the fragile green survived it"

~ *W.S Merwin, from* The Vixen

Part One

THE APPLE

So this is the fruit that made us all human.
So this is the fruit we reached for and got.
So this is the fruit that ripens in autumn.

⁂

Cezanne,
I envy your eye.
Knowing roundness,
you put an apple in a bowl,
curve into curve
like lovers.

Mother,
you sliced the green ones for pie,
steaming like morning on the sill.

Doctor,
the apple I eat to keep you away
is the shape, the weight of a heart.

⁂

Long before the child, reaching up to pick,
before the ladder in the branches,
long before the tree, full in our yard,
a farmer rests
in the shade of his team.

Their dark sides shine.
In summer's last heat,
in the field's long work,
the apple he's saved
is cold on his teeth.

    ⊪   *

Shine an apple on your pants.
Make the apple genie dance.

Rub him, rub him, into life.
Ask him for a loving wife.

And for children I'd ask next,
talismans for the witch's hex.

One more wish is all that's left.
Beg him for eternal breath.

    ⊪   *

Quartered,
a seed rocks
in each tiny cradle.

Like blood,
in the air an apple
rusts.

SPLITTING WOOD

When I lift my ax,
this fist on the end of a stick,
bring it thumping down
on the stump of an oak,
a door in the earth opens.

I step down into darkness,
mold and cellar musk.

The grub grins from his perch.

I hear the roots sucking
like hearts.

A furnace burns at the end of a shadow—
this dark pantry of heat!

Hello, bone,
sweet tooth of the dog.
And you, acorn,
the squirrel's dried fruit.

Warm here
below the frost line
I am brother to the mole,
the bear
wheezing all winter in his cave.

THE NEST

Found in the limbs by my son
walking the wind in the apple
the reach and hold of his climbing
the fluttering down of leaves

Held in his palm to the house
a hollow of woven reeds
of hair from the rubbings of deer
skin from the shed of a snake

Set by his bed on the bureau
by the wash of ocean in shells
the husk of a locust still singing
the silent horn of a snail

Heard in his sleep as song
a bird as bright as blood
pecking the breath from blossoms
to feed the beaks of its young

THE WELL

The mystery of water underground,
the dark stream where the dead kneel
cupping their pale hands,
splashing the stillness from their eyes.

I drop a stone in ours to hear
if there's water for the children's bath.
And if it's dry, no sound—the pebble
a star, falling through the night.

Here, a rope once hung, a bucket
on its noose. Here, the cattle gathered
summer evenings at the trough,
their dull heads bowed.

No one fishes this hole, or ever did,
though in the cold, moonless pools
fins move through the dark, deep
in the ground, where spawning begins.

ICE

If the earth
in its waking
remembers rain, grass,
the scent of flowers,

then in its sleep
it dreams of ice,
of wind again
across the glacier

the way we hear
winter nights
when sound
travels for miles:

in the distance,
the scraping of stones;
through the thin air,
a father's voice.

THE ICEHOUSE

Where the puckerbrush snags your lure
along the west side of the lake
is where the icehouse stood, black with wet
in the sweat of summer, glistening all winter.
I cast to the pilings rising like masts
from the water, from the mist, and see the breath
of horses dragging blades, their muscled thighs—
hear the men in rubber aprons, slick as fish,
cursing the blocks, the cold, prodding each piece
with their spikes to the shore. All afternoon
the clank, the hiss of the belt lifting
chunk after chunk through the winter light
to its dark bed of hay in this place
of black timber, this ship rising like a dream
through the sand, through the rock, its hold
cradling silver, cooling the fruit of summer.

BUILDING THE POND

In the ravine
the maples lean to the light
like sunflowers
and fall to my saw
like weeds.

Since morning,
blue smoke, whine,
the rasp of clearing.
I sit by a stump,
exhausted.

In the afternoon light
the silence of sawdust
drifting through air
as if through water,
oarlocks banging overhead,
the splash of a paddle.

It is spring as I cast
where I've cut all day,
the bass on their nests.
From twelve feet down,
bubbles of trapped air.

To sleep is to find
what lies on the bottom,
that lake you fished as a kid,
the log you snagged
in the deep water.

THE RITUAL

The first night of frost
we all have our chores,
the children in the garden
picking tomatoes
hard as apples;
in their mother's hands,
the final flowers.
I hood in plastic
what plants I can
and as the wind stills
lug in wood,
stacking oak against the dark
the clearest night of the year.

The first night of frost
we go to bed early,
the children at their prayers,
in the darkness
their soft words;
my wife in her slippers
going up the stairs.
I open the window
and smell the air,
hear as I hold her
in the warmth of our bed
a dog bark, far off,
under the stars.

THE COMPASS

Each fall with a stone
I drive a stake
by the well in our yard,

a hardwood pole
chiseled sharp
I stab in the earth's

cold heart—
a steady point
in the blowing white

where tracks fill fast
and sleep comes on
like finding home.

STONES

The endless movement of stones,
how they work their way up,
surface each spring in the garden
as if out of breath.

How others will sink,
slowly, over the years, unnoticed,
like a man at peace
slipping off to sleep, or dying.

History happens under our feet,
the tunneling of worms,
the loosening of earth
letting breathe

what's underneath—
the cold foreheads crowning like birth,
our footsteps each year
heavier, deeper.

NORTH

Up here, in this cold,
you won't get fat.

I don't mean your ribs,
I mean your words.

Far north, in the deep snow,
nouns are skin and bone

for verbs to gnaw on,
lean as ice, raw as oak—

cut, clear; split, burn—
one breath, one bite

up here where ax
is both a thing and work.

BACK ROAD

Winter mornings
driving past
I'd see these kids
huddled like grouse
in the plowed ruts
in front of their shack
waiting for the bus,
three small children
bunched against the drifts
rising behind them.

This morning
I slowed to wave
and the smallest,
a stick of a kid
draped in a coat,
grinned and raised
his red, raw hand,
the snowball
packed with rock
aimed at my face.

Bruce Guernsey

STRAY

A dog I have never seen
howls each night
outside my window.

He has no body,
no shadow to track him by
in the dark, nothing
to hurl a rock at.

I have snuck out in slippers,
waited by bones for hours
in the cool night,
each picked clean as stars
when I woke, shivering.

For evidence the pound
needs more than a voice—
the breed, a tuft of fur—
will not answer after five
as if dogs in the dark
did not exist.

But each night
as I drift into dream
gripping a stone,
I know he'll call,
that howl
hollow as a bowl.

TOAD

The mad uncle
nobody loves but the children.
How they squeal as he dances
hatless
in the rain.

The frog is a prince,
elegant
in his emerald jacket—
the toad, a jester,
his coat of warts, brown motley.

Once, before time,
the toad had a beautiful voice,
sang all evening
in the grass—
sang so sweetly that birds
pecked the music from his throat.

All the songs of birds
are the toad's
hopping at the feet of kids
for laughs,
the old soft-shoe.

THE DUMP PICKERS

On Sundays
carting my trash to the dump
I'd see them swarming
the piles like gnats,
a whole family of pickers
straight from Mass:
Dad's suit, white
as the noon sky, Junior
in a polka-dot tie—
in bright, patent leathers
his small, pale sister.

From the highest of piles
Mother shouted orders
through a paper cup,
the men hurrying under
her red, high heels,
dragging metal to the pickup,
the little girl giggling,
spinning on her toes
through the blowing paper
like a dancer, a little twist
of wind in the dust.

JUNE TWENTY-FIRST

My mother's cigarette flares and fades,
the steady pulse of a firefly,
on the patio under the chestnut.

The next door neighbors are over.
My father, still slender, is telling a joke:
laughter jiggles in everyone's drinks.

On his hour's reprieve from sleep,
my little brother dances
in the sprinkler's circle of water.

At fourteen, I'm too old
to run naked with my brother,
too young to laugh with my father.

I stand there with my hands in my pockets.
The sun refuses to set,
bright as a penny in a loafer.

Bruce Guernsey

MILK

When I was a boy
there was music to milk in the morning,
its windy ring, the bottles clinking
like chimes in the dark
when I'd wake before school
to hear the milkman bringing
on his white wings our milk
thick with cream for the licking.

From the tin box on the back stoop
I'd lift them slippery as fish still dripping
cool against my small boy's chest, hugging
glass to the white, icebox door,
my morning chore before the nuns,
those angels on broom-sticks over me hovering
asking why, *why God made thee,*
their steel-rimmed eyes and me, still yawning.

Milk, oh milk, sweet, sweet milk,
it melts a winter morning
this milk I warm for my kids, this soothing
silk from the carton with its faces now
of the missing, vague in wax, everybody's children
who late for the school bell's ringing
took a ride one day forever.
The bus, kids, it's here. I love you, get going.

THE BLIND CAVEFISH

In my tank, that eight-gallon world
I governed like a god,
turning the light on or off at will,
the Neon Tetras darted all day,
an iridescence of green and blue;
in schools of silver stripes
the Zebras never slowed down
except at night and in the morning
zipped around the Angel Fish
with its trailing fins of lace,
attendants to a graceful bride.

Guppies, snails, a fat pair
of Black Mollies always mating,
algae like moss, plants with Latin names
only a priest could pronounce,
their vines like tentacles
in and out the gingerbread house
with its bubbling chimney pumping air,
a Hansel and Gretel place
where the Blind Cavefish,
shy, pale, vulnerable in the light, would hide.

After school, in my attic room,
I'd eclipse the sun of this tiny world,
pull the shades and sit by the tank, alone.
The thrill in my blood, even now,
feeling him stir,

his slow nudging through the door,
his caution, then growing ease
the way I'd wait, first afraid,
then slipping into sleep
with fins through the darkness,
for centuries in caves,
my eyes sealed over, without a trace,
the night as palpable as waves
and light, some ancient dream.

LEAVING THE STATION

The tug of starting.
I watch the windows
on the other track,
the flash of their lights
through the station's dark.
We back into evening,
my face on the glass.

The car is warm
and in its rocking
I hear my grandfather,
long since dead,
shuffling cards,
the soft applause
of their falling together.

This is his last trip south.
He knows he is dying
but can't remember the rules
or whose deal.
He shuffles, restacks,
shuffles again,
nodding his head with the rails.

FLYING HOME

I.

Stepping from the cab
I leap a puddle to the sidewalk,
holding tight a bag of grapefruit
brighter than the sun.
November in Florida:
the day is dark and thick.
My grandfather,
who kept us all in shoes as kids
and mailed galoshes every fall, is dead.

sixty years we were married
so short   so short

I wait in line with my bags
and remember the weight
of my grandmother's arm,
holding her yesterday at the funeral:
that soft dimpled flesh.
They pack my fruit
in a special crate.

sixty years   so short

Her white face was powdered pink.
In the sun that refused to shine,
I noticed
she is nearly bald and wears a wig.

sixty years of happiness
so short

I hurry aboard

and search for a seat.
At lunch yesterday,
five of us sat at a table for six.

II.
The attendant
brings today's paper
and smiles
like an undertaker.

I order a drink,
a double,
and the news begins to spin.

Flying through the air
with the greatest of ease
having to pee
at ten thousand feet.

sixty years   sixty years
so short

Drunk in my seat
I stare out the window
for my grandfather
knowing he's here,
in the light,
and fall asleep.

III.
From the bright, pure air
we drop into dark weather.

I sit next to the exit,
terrified of landings.

His bronze casket hovers
at the earth like the sun.

Home in just three hours!
so short   so short

We close our eyes
and the wheels touch.

Part Two

A SPECIAL PROVIDENCE

Fall. At my doorstep I find
hurled there like the paper
lying beside it, a sparrow,
its twig of a neck snapped,
a bubble of blood on its beak.
I lift it by its wishbone
of a wing and see as I do
in the storm-door window
I put up last week
a sky without wind, fresh
and deep as water in wells,
orchards of bright red leaves
etched against its blue,
see this bird, gliding
with a song into this world
of glass sky and tree.

HIGH FLYING

In the living room
in his jump-seat
my son
hangs from the branch
of the door sill
asleep, a pilot
slumped in his parachute.

Unstrapping the limp,
vulnerable body
I lift him to bed
on the rough
stretcher of my arms—
easy, easy now—
as a medic the wounded.

He stirs once
to reassure me
and returns, weary
from a day
of high flying, of singing
so close to heaven,
unaware of the world's weight
and yet to learn
the brutal power of flight.

AERIAL PHOTOGRAPH

Staring down
at this black
and white shot
taken by no one
I ever knew,
this stark photo
of the place I grew up
way out in the country,
I feel the sudden
vertigo of dreams,
the tumbling, twisting
terror of being
high above
and falling,
the blue-green blur
of earth and air,
the frantic grasping,
my voice a torn chute,
trailing . . .

and on the ground, a stillness,
the fields pieced neatly in squares,
the perfectly parallel rows of corn,
the right angle lines of fence;

in the picture's center, two rectangles:
a roof inside a yard where a boy,
alone in this geometry, is staring up
at something he sees, the plane perhaps, and waving.

DISTANCE

There is a house across the field.

From the other side where I started
it did not seem so far away.

I have been walking toward it a long time,
through mud, the turned ground,
and now this snow beginning to fall.

The house has grown
only slightly larger
and I think I see someone outside.

Yes, I am sure of it—
people, two or three, beside the house,
moving about.

I am waving, suddenly waving,
but out so far in this openness of field
will not be seen or heard.

Faster, walk faster,
before they go inside
whoever they are, before they close the door
across the field
where nothing is growing,
the gray, flat horizon.

OCTOBER

Today, they're cutting the corn,
the stalks dry and blowing, brown
and rattling, rattling
when you walk by
as if something were inside,
a deer, a coon, something
alive, someone maybe.
But today
they're cutting it down
as they do every October,
the combines on the back roads,
on the fields,
working all night, next day and next,
until the land is flat again
and we can see
some ranch house we forgot
a mile or so away.
Out here
the corn is a special mystery,
a haunted place
where children warned not to
want to play.
No wonder each September
before the harvest
some farm kid disappears,
losing himself in the tall acres,
tunneling under the sabers
rattling over his head,

vanishes for hours, for days.
Usually, they come back
or are found; once in a while,
they're not. That's why
slowing to a walk
somewhere out from home
and out of breath,
I always stop, sure I've heard
something in there,
something I woke jogging by,
one of those kids maybe
in the forest of corn,
hear him, the closer I get,
running away.

MY FATHER'S VOICE

A bad connection,
my father's voice, thin on the phone,
but there were no storms back east,
none here in Illinois.

He was winded,
though it rang just once,
as if he'd been running—
said he was waiting for a business call.

The less I could hear him,
the louder I yelled,
sounding like him those Saturday mornings,
shouting out chores.

I asked would he be out this fall
but his answer was lost in voices,
far off, some other phone.
In the distance, I could hear their laughter.

SMOKE

From his window on the ward
I watch it puff from the hospital stack,
black and billowing,
vanishing far across the fields,

and wonder is it coal or oil
thickening the thin fall air.
Five floors up, I'm glad for glass
and wind that blows the stench away

though in the seasonless ether of this place
I crave the smell of burning leaves,
to sit again on the damp, raked grass
and watch my father cupping a match.

He is kneeling to the leaves,
the reds, the yellows, the orange leaves,
the smoke in whispers first
soon full with the breath of fall,

the rhythm of his arms and rake
ghostlike through the gray.
Then, in the swirling haze, he disappears,
slips away to circle back

where I'm waiting there afraid,
searching the smoke for my father—
a hide-and-seek he liked to play
every fall the same, sneaking up behind me

from where he was hiding,
coming back always, like some kind of magic
a boy could believe, from nowhere,
like a promise he would never die.

MAPS

Those who've been to war love maps.
They keep them everywhere: in pockets, drawers,
the glove box of cars and stacked by the toilet.
Maps are what they read, these poems for soldiers
who hear in the lines the whir of blades,
who smell in the colors the char of smoke.

They know the hidden meaning of rivers,
the true symbol of water, how dry a last breath—
that here, spread flat on the kitchen table,
are really mountains, the strategic home of gods.
For those such as these, myth is truth,
and this paper you touch, a metaphor for earth.

THE LOST BRIGADE

My Uncle Donald always knew the weather.
"Had to, during the war," he told me, "in Alaska,"
as we stood on the steps of our cabin in New Hampshire,
this strange, middle-aged man and I,
scanning the skies for Zeroes—
"I hear 'em. Doncha? Doncha, through the clouds?"—
but I heard nothing, saw only the lake, its surface
the color of pewter before a storm, and my uncle
cupping his troubled brow with his hands
like a soldier with field glasses, his blue eyes blank
and far, far away.

He'd been a member, I learned years later,
of "The Lost Brigade," the men shipped to the Arctic
in 1942 to guard the Aleutians, those stepping-stones
the ancient Asians crossed centuries ago,
and on Umnak Island Uncle Don gazed west for months
toward Kiska, the island base of the Japanese
fifty miles away.

Taking turns in twelve-hour shifts,
he and the others of "The Lost Brigade" stared across an
        open tundra
seemingly forever, watching for cracks, some small fracture
in the steel-gray weld of sea and sky, blinded finally
by all they did not see, like the farmers out here in Illinois
after weeks of plowing the empty, late fall fields,
staring into their coffee, silent, numbed
by so much nothing. Forgotten on Umnak for nearly two
        years,
Private Donald Heffernan went insane, had to be shipped

back to the States, and by the state,
put away.

        "He saw God's foot on the treadle of the Loom,"
Melville says of Pip, the cabin-boy swept from the Pequod
into the sea, gone mad from that immensity. And my uncle?—
a priest without beads, mumbling to himself, an old man now
in his dead parents' house on St. Pete Beach
where he's piled a fort of old papers
deep as snow on any tundra, and boarded up the doors.
From there last week, hurricane season, they dragged him off
screaming about devils in the distance
to a locked ward at the Florida V.A., a room without windows.
Donald's had enough of sky
though he knows the weather, the gathering clouds
a squadron's thunder
so far away.

NIGHT PATROL

My father never slept real well after the war
and as my mother tells, he woke in fear
so deep, so far away, he seemed to stare
straight out at nothing she could see or hear.

Or worse—she wraps her robe around her, remembering—
he'd sit there grinning, bolt upright beside her,
this mad look on his face, the bed springs quivering
with some hilarity the night had whispered.

And once, "He did this your father, I swear he did—
he must have been still dreaming, rest his soul—
he tried to close my frightened eyes, my lids,
to thumb them shut like he was on patrol

the way he'd learned so they would sleep, the dead.
And then he blessed himself and bowed his head."

RADIO DAYS

My father ate his breakfast standing up,
cupping a bowl of cereal in his hand,
at attention by the kitchen counter
where the radio crackled with news from Korea.
We had no television then, few families did
south of Boston in '52,
so what we knew came through the Emerson
with its vibrating wooden case and rotary dial
for the short wave band, fading
in and out from overseas.
At night, I'd cart the old crate
up to my bedroom for the Red Sox-
Yankees game, closing my eyes
to better imagine each play
through the gunfire of static,
waking hours later to dead air.
"Who won?" I'd ask my dad in the morning
as he stood by the radio
with his eyes closed, too,
but to a different kind of field.

Six years home from the war
he never said a word about it,
even the day the letter came
asking him to volunteer
the way Ted Williams did.
"I can't," was all he said,
and that night after the game

I climbed the empty stairs to the attic
where the secret box with all his Army gear
hummed in my dream like a distant station.
I order you to turn it off!—"I can't,"
and into the radio's halo of light,
suddenly swinging a splintered bat,
my father stabbed and stabbed and stabbed,
fans everywhere yelling, blood-wet and spilling
out of the wound onto a field
littered with helmets and paper.
I lay awake for hours after,
and in the morning, dutifully carried
the magic crystal down, and for my father
adjusted the dial, finding the picture.

THE SCOUT

Just another beggar kid
in the cinders and soot
outside Belgrade, working the train I took
through Yugoslavia to Greece
the winter we were shelling Iraq—

like so many I'd seen each stop, these strays
walking the tracks, window to window,
palms up, filthy as the roadside snow,
no more than nine or ten years old,
scavenging for cigarettes.

But this one, this kid, this kid and his cap,
a Davy Crockett coonskin cap
complete with ringed tail, amazing!—this boy
with his frontier hat, on his own
in the crush of crowd, the blowing paper.

Leaning out the double glass I see the widows
heavy on their canes, a few old men
in dark suits and everywhere soldiers,
groups of them all over, smoking, pacing,
rechecking their orders—and there,

darting in between them all,
the bad boy, the bandit, that young pioneer—
the soldiers like older brothers
he scoots around as they grab, laughing,
for his pelt of hair, but in the lurch

and screech of steel, the hiss of steam
as we start south to the sea, he slips their grasp
and coon-tail waving, escapes
behind the black and red graffiti sprayed
like war paint on the station's wall,

out of the wind, lighting up.

ME AND HITLER AT THE RHINE

The first time I ever saw my father
was in a picture he sent from the war.
"This is your Dad," my mother said,
and I searched through the rubble fallen like blocks.
There, on the turret of a tank, a man was laughing,
holding on to some statue's head, a head
with no body, marble and grim,
a bottle raised in his other hand.
"Me and Hitler at the Rhine,"
my mother read, laughing too and crying
at my father's words on the back.
She was glad the war was over.

I saw my father for the last time today
and late, after the crying, the laughter,
I wake in the warm night to thunder,
to the sound of shells, the rumbling of a tank,
the walls, our whole house shaking, this house
my mother's now alone, the endless halls.
In the lightning, sudden on the ceiling like a searchlight,
I can see the statue rise, massive and stiff—
in my chest can hear it marching, marching, in strict steps
striding toward the river now,
its right hand out and rigid,
a man's head in its marble hand.

SHAVING WITHOUT A MIRROR

As I shave him in bed
he stares at me from the pillow,
towel tucked under the chin, mouth
a dark spot in the lather—

stares the way I do
at myself in the morning,
the way I did watching him
sharpen his razor on a belt.

The slap and ring of steel on leather—
how careful he had to be
following the ridge of his chin
in the sunlit mirror.

I turn his head. The scrape
of razor, flecks of beard
I wipe on the towel.
On the neck, a nick of blood.

THE SEARCH

I.

Every night since you disappeared
almost a year ago now
I wake around 3:00
and lie here like this
staring at nothing,
and think of those nights last spring
you spent outside alone,
where you went, what you did
as the searchers circled in with lights,
the howl of their trail hounds on the leash,
Nazis, I'll be to your blurred mind
as you blundered through the honeysuckle vines,
after me, following, still after me, running, stumbling,
the war you never stopped fighting.

Or did they even come close
to where you fell, to where you shivered,
to where you'd wandered off that sweet May morning
from your ward at the V.A.?—
the tremors of Parkinson's disease
shaking the voice I once feared,
your cries for help, mute, confused,
lost in the stars you stared up at
from some field or thicket snare,
no clouds to blanket the earth's heat,
no ceiling like this one over my head,
this blankness I've come to know, to hate.

II.

No wonder we believe in ghosts.
Where else do our shadows go in the dark,
putting on someone else's clothes,
dressing up to haunt us?

Mother,
I don't want his winter coat.
I know you'd just bought it,
that he only wore it once.
I know it will fit me fine.
I know, I know, I know.

Mother,
Don't send it please.

III.

For the buried, closure.
For the missing, space—

this Illinois distance
where a man can walk forever,
stubble and sky,
where a house on the other side
is ever the horizon.

The missing need a place to be,
as much as for themselves as we

who cannot rest for tracking them, we
who dream of snow, his footprints fresh and he
just ahead I'm sure, just over the next rise, see
where he stumbled here, how he needs
an arm, a place to lean,
faster now, hurry, hurry please,

then suddenly to wake and the ground
winter-bare, hard,
the snow, the tracking snow
a passing dream.

IV.

To hunt is to know,
to be the deer itself,
to freeze at the snap of a branch,
vanish at the flash of a shadow.

So I'll put on his shoes, his shirt,
I'll wrap myself in his scent
and some spring day by being him
I'll find out where on earth he went.

Canvas, this damp air like canvas:
this melting
the rich, wet smell of a tent.
Tulips, crocus, the long necks of iris.

Over there, what's that? What's that
I hear across the lawns, beyond the grounds?—
the scraping rattle of a rake.
Ah, these hands of mine, this endless

shake, shake, shake.
I crave the oak of handles,
to make a fist again,
to grip a hammer, shovel, pick—

and across the grass,
the new-raked hospital grass,
he shuffled toward the sound of work
and never came back.

V.

Pressing my thumb to my wrist
I count the tiny sheep
leaping there, beat by beat,
minutes, hours, morning,
and remember
teaching my son to tell time,
the big hand, the small,
the numbers slipping from them,
eight, nine, ten.

Drifting off,
I find my father with his sleeves rolled
driving a stake with a stone.

FROM RAIN

I hear him say in some far field,
watch how the shadow falls
in a circle on the ground.

THE CAP

On the third day without sleep
I woke from a waking dream
since dreams were the same as waking
and put on my father's cap, blaze-orange
across the corn fields, through the hedgerows
like a small fire in the cold
those mornings we hunted together

and searched that morning alone, certain
I'd find him that day, remembering
a pheasant we'd shot and lost
somewhere in the brush,
thirty, forty yards away, not far
but gone, not even a feather,
just gone, like my father
until I set his cap in the center
the way he showed me how,

circling outward from it ever further,
fields, trees, years from then now
where I left it that night
that he might find it, still warm
from the dream I had while searching,
from the search I make each day,
still circling.

NAMING THE TREES

At the national cemetery in Gettysburg
all the trees have names,
both the family and genus
on small brass plaques at the base of each
to let the visitor know
the kind of oak,
whether red, white or black,
and is this rock or silver maple
looking once like any other
burlapped ball of roots
when it was lowered to earth
those decades after the war.

Colorful names like Tulip Poplar,
Weeping Beech, Buckeye,
Sweet Gum and Ginko—
sounding like nicknames almost, these trees
from every region and state
with broad leaves or skinny,
shiny, dull, or no leaves at all
like the Eastern Hemlock,
but all, all with names every one,
no matter the size and shape
amidst the many anonymous
mute stones in their shade.

Bruce Guernsey

SOLDIER'S HOME

September 30, 1865

Dear Luther,

I wonder if you've made it back by now,
up there to New Hampshire,
and if you had a trip as grand as mine,
'cause did I ever!—
the big parade with Sarge in Pittsburgh
and Willy showing me the town of Cleveland.
What a time on the railway, too,
the B&O, and tipped my cap to everyone,
I felt so proud in uniform and then
to see the brand-new silver tracks
out-stretching on and on, all shiny
clear to the Wabash, imagine!

And just across,
like I promised when you come,
there it was on the breeze again, the corn smell
sweeter than a lady's parlor
as down our lane I marched, the dust
whirling about like ever
but not so red like in Virginia
though it was just like being there,
he scared me so,
my father with his holler like a Reb
with me in his sights before I saw him
way up on the corn crib,

then Mama's damn crying
brushing the war off my wools
with her handkerchief, working the buttons bright
like it was inspection.

But when I stripped back down
and donned my same old coveralls
to sit the sunset on the stoop alone
while Ma cleaned up from supper
(made my favorites, chops with applesauce)
and Papa at the evening chores—
I mean, what with the whippoorwills
and blowing about of the wheat, I have to know
was what we did real, Luke?—
the rivers we crossed and washed in,
the tents and mud and waiting for boots?
Remember that?—and the first time
we heard their yell, how it sent a chill
and their always coming at us?—
and then last spring, all those yellow flowers
on the Blue Ridge hills?

But tomorrow,
tomorrow we'll be picking and hauling
because the corn, why it's ready now, all dried
like when I left but like I never did,
each year, the cutting and plowing,
then how it all grows back like coming home.

I hope the perch are thick in Goose Pond

the way you said they were and bragged upon.
Catch a mess for me
though I've never seen one, a perch.
Lots of work along Lake Erie, Will says.
Maybe I'll try come winter.
What about you?

We all went off and saw so much, didn't we,
but I got no one near to tell it to.
Hope you do.
Anymore,
it's so quiet here.

Most sincerely, your friend,

William "Billy" Eyrse
Corporal
4th Brigade, 2nd Division, 5th Corps
First Illinois Volunteers

DOUG

When my father came home from the war
two years after I was born
I couldn't match his voice with his picture
and cried each time he came near.

Learning to talk, I called him "Doug,"
the way my mother did,
this strange man who tried so hard to hold me—
how could he be my dad?

My father was there, right there in black and white
over my bed every morning
where I could see him with his uniform on,
boarding a train, waving good-by and smiling,

not that deep voice down the hall,
not those footsteps outside my door.
No, my dad's a soldier who'll be home soon,
so watch out you, whoever you are.

Then Doug went away like him,
leaving for work before dawn,
the knocker on the front door always tapping
as he closed it behind him in the dark,

the big brass knocker that brought me running
to peer through the mail slot
for him who never knocked, who never came,
only Doug, home late

each night from work, this man Doug
tiptoeing into my room,
without a word come to cover me,
stepping down from the train.

THE BIRTHMARK

No matter what he did—
the Silver Cross for valor,
the powder he'd cover
his right cheek with
like gauze on a wound,
his Florida tan—no matter,
his was a mask he couldn't take off,
rising like flame from the collar
of his tropical shirt
everyone noticed first,

my Uncle Charles
with the map on his face
as he called it,
to not get lost, so he said,
my baby sister giggling,
bouncing on his knee
each Christmas
when he'd come to visit,
his bags full of presents
as he reached to hug me
and I ran away,
afraid to touch it,
the burn from birth
that made Charles different,

though when I did once,
sneaking up

where he slept on our couch,
it felt the same
to my tender hand
as my father's face
after he shaved, my uncle
like my sister in her crib
sound asleep as I traced
the scarlet coast for his house,
my fingers trembling, barely touching,
not wanting to hurt him anymore.

THE FISHERMAN

When asked where I learned to fish
by those on the stream
admiring my back cast in the trees
or, on rare occasion, the fly landing where I wish,

I'd like to blame my father
as any good son would do, but can't—
the old guy had no patience for it
nor did he give two cents for water

other than something he had to cross over
on his relentless pursuit of the other side
where he might make some money on a sale.
No, it was from his ne'er-do-well brother

I got so good at cussing
the branches hungry for my fly,
my Uncle Alfred, who always had the time
and whose casting never touched the brush

under which he'd float his feathered hook
where he knew a good one finned
the current swirling white around
the jagged angles of a rock

jutting through the surface bubbling
where a trout has left
its shadow deep and leapt
through light but faster, my uncle hooting,

his line suddenly tight with the music
all fisherman love, the wild leaps
of a rainbow on a run and whee
of the singing reel, your heart gone spastic.

How I loved to watch Uncle Al
who other times became so quiet and sad
when he wasn't out there with a rod in his hand,
doing the one thing he did so well

though once the best shot in this county,
my father said, who did love to hunt,
but Alfred wouldn't go anymore, his guns
he'd swapped for gear and a little money,

enough to get him by for a while,
never keeping a job very long,
used cars and clothing stores no river's song
he'd hum to himself, almost smiling,

who in the war had killed a man
with those clear eyes of his, taking aim,
the same eyes that through a thicket of pine
could drop a grouse, the same hands

I watched let go a whopper brookie
after he wet them in the river.
"Always do that, remember.
Trout don't have scales. Wasn't that some beauty!"

FORTUNATE SONS

My Uncle Sheldon never went to war,
the oldest son exempt by law
to carry on our family name,
to care for the farm.
From milking cows his hands grew strong
those cold, Catskill mornings,
and gentle, too, bathed in milk,
his fingers long against the firm,
pink udders, and by the time his brothers
came back from overseas,
he'd taught himself to play the piano.

His brothers—
Alfred, Douglas, Charles—
he calmed with those hands
when they'd wake in their beds like boys
to the high whine of shells
and brute fact of lead,
the rhythm, like milking, of his fingers at the keys
stilling the rattling windows
with music like steam, grassy and sweet
from the buckets rising, filling with sleep
the house they each were born in.

Part Three

ICE FISHING

When the doctor beams his line of light
in the water of your eye,
can he see the stars, the glisten of your tears?

I pull a bluegill from the dark,
its belly pink, the winter moon.
On the ice, it flops just once.

The eye of a fish is flat
for seeing under water. Out here, in air,
nothing it sees has depth.

Summers, the pond a sky,
you can't see in because of the light.
All you see is sky.

This afternoon it's ten below,
the land, the ice I fish through, white.
I stare in the hole, jigging the line.

IGLOO

For a door
the eye of a telescope.
Within,
the infinite galaxies of snow,
cinders for stars.

In this roundness
the dog alone
circling his spot
can sleep.
The rest of us?—
insomniacs,
searching for corners.

The only window,
a hole for fire.
The startled explorers,
their tracks
filling with snow,
seeing the smoke.

Those shadows on the wall
bending over the flame,
that flickering of hands
on the endless wall.
Listen,
their lips are moving
but not a word.

Bruce Guernsey

WEATHERSTRIPPING

Outside my daughter
is rolling a snowman
while in among dolls
and posters of Pink Floyd,
heady from a new perfume
from an aunt at Christmas,
I weatherstrip her bedroom window.

Still chunky, she busily shapes
the year's first snow
into an image she has in her mind
from some childhood story:
round, rollicking, ever happy in his top-hat,
everybody's granddad,

but as I watch through the steam
of my breath on the pane,
I remember the razor
I found in the shower this morning,
its new edge packed with soap
and nubs of hair like down.

The snow is falling lightly now again
and my daughter at her work
begins to blur and the snowman
to take a young man's shape,
to reach an arm out for her,
to ease her toward him.

From Rain

With my thumb I pack the stripping tight
where cold is seeping in her room.
"Megan," I tap at the glass, "Megan, come in,"
but in the whirling afternoon
he holds her slender form against him hard
and she, gently firm,
takes his whiteness onto her.

ICE STORM

To go to bed one April night,
a halo around the moon,
to sleep for hours it seems,
so soundly
you never heard the sleet—

to waken so suddenly old,
all that green gone white,
the orchard creaking,
its branches brittle as ribs—

to squint at the light with milky eyes,
the great-grandchildren gathered near,
all staring, all frightened—

to point toward the window,
someone wetting your lips—

to try to tell them

OATMEAL

In the cold kitchen
before school,
my mother spooning steam
into our bowls—

upstairs her father
waits in a bib,
his teeth like ice
in a glass by the bed.

MOSS

How must it be
to be moss,
that slipcover of rocks?
Imagine,

greening in the dark,
longing for north,
the silence
of birds gone south.

How does moss do it,
all day
in a dank place
and never a cough?—

a wet dust
where light fails,
where the chisel
cut the name.

YAM

The potato that ate all its carrots,
can see in the dark like a mole,

its eyes the scars
from centuries of shovels, tines.

May spelled backwards
because it hates the light,

pawing its way, padding along,
there in the catacombs.

GLASS

is the wind's half-brother,
born of Touch,
their promiscuous mother,
old, blind in her bed,
lusting for Silence,

that lover of flesh,
who took her one night
in an ecstasy of gesture,

like what I see
when the wind invisibly
tosses the branches
outside my window,
cold and silent.

SIGN LANGUAGE

The old couple I heard about
on this morning's news,

deaf mutes
in a burning tenement,

the whorls of their hands
at the frozen windows—

gestures
born of the wind,

that shaper of smoke,
carrier of scent.

The deaf learn fear
from the thrashing of leaves;

from their stillness,
prayer.

THE HANDS

The only time we touch now
is in our sleep, as if our hands,
finding each other,
have lives of their own.

Joined to our surprise every morning,
they are full of longing,
like a one-armed man
trying to pray.

We pull them apart
starting the day, yours
to your work, mine to mine:
purses, pockets, change.

How they love the night,
the cool of linen, the underside
of pillows—sneaking out,
meeting without us in the dark.

Theirs is a language we've forgotten,
a way of speaking now their own:
touching, whispering,
making plans.

LONG DISTANCE

Suppose your wife should call
suddenly fluent in a strange language,
you couldn't understand a word.
Would you know it was her?

There's nothing but silence to go on,
the pauses she makes.
You've slept beside her for years—
you know her breathing.

In sleep, the voice is free of words,
like traveling without luggage.
We reach the kingdom of mutes.
Listen now through the long cord.

THE LETTER X

Poor X,
never the treasure,
only the spot,
the anonymous name
on some illiterate's will.

Could Xerxes play the xylophone?—
the Z's got X's tongue,
and when it speaks in its own voice
your X
is on the phone.

In the assassin's scope,
the body made simple—
where your arms meet your legs,
the heart.
X,

oh thou swaddled, illegitimate child,
confess!
'twas you in the manger that Xmas.
And there, too, on Calvary,
the shadow of the crucifix.

THE EYE CHART

And if these lines
were all that was left,

all cookbooks, histories,
poetry charred,

some future
archaeologist

wiping the dust
from this plastic chart,

sounding out
the backwards letters,

speaking
the large ones loud,

his voice ever softer
line after line—

little, less, nothing,
squinting at the silence.

GRADING PAPERS

His essay said:
"In Vietnam
a common (though discouraged)
practice for Marines
is to hack-off V-C ears
which they send home
or keep
for souvenirs."

The comment
in the margin read:
"Subject of the clause
should be its referent.
I'd put this
in the passive voice."

LOUIS B. RUSSELL

Louis B. Russell, a shop teacher from Indianapolis, died
Wednesday after living for more than six years with a trans-
planted heart—longer than anyone else in history. . . . He had
received the heart of a 17-year-old boy killed in a hunting
accident. —The Associated Press

At night
he'd lie in bed
listening
to his new heart thump,
the blood pumping like strong legs
in a race
around the body's track,
its quick steps the echo
of his own young heart
as he reached for her hand
years ago,
that first kiss.

And falling asleep
he'd dream of the rifle, lifting it
slowly, slowly
to his cheek,
his heart wild with death:
his first buck
square in the crosshairs
as he squeezes forever the blue steel

of the trigger,
his own head in another's sights
exploding like a melon
under the blood-bright cap.

Suddenly awake,
he'd listen for hours to the clock's tick
quick as a sprinter's breath,
its bright circle of numbers
grinning in the dark,
and think
of the shop class he'd teach tomorrow,
the powerful young men,
hammers
tight in their fists.

THE SKULL

My neighbor, a doctor, keeps a skull
in his study over his books perched there
like a raven, a real human skull
complete with filled, yellow teeth,
is cracked jaw clamped shut like some fat lady's
desperate to lose weight. With shelves
for shoulders, it just sits there
collecting dust on its shellacked, bald top,
my neighbor's four kids and delicious wife
watched by those hollow sockets each day.
"Jay," I finally asked, "why do you keep
that awful gargoyle up there anyway?"
My neighbor smiled one of those weird,
faraway surgeon's smiles and handed
me the head saying, "Hold it to your ear
and you can hear the ocean."

Bruce Guernsey

THE AFFAIR

Into the party on a trapeze
she uses no net.
The air around her is filled
with jugglers' bright rings.
Of all the girls you've ever met
she looks best in leopard skin.

But wait—
for her next trick,
she swallows a sword of fire.
Clever girl,
riding your boredom bareback.

With the flash of a smile
she stuffs your wife, your kids,
into a tall black hat
and pulls herself out instead.
"Yes," you cry, "Yes!"
and she saws you in half.

THE BOOMERANG

To hold these abstract wings
is to feel the glide of the falcon—
the curve of this beakless bone,
flight itself in your hand.

I bought my son a toy one,
showed him how in the yard.
The whistle it makes going out
behind us suddenly coming back.

In the distance William Tell
could see it make its turn,
placed an apple on his head
and shook while standing still.

The efficiency of a war
fought with boomerangs!
No enemy needed, no weapons lost,
no report of survivors.

ONCE UPON A TIME

"... and he fell into a deep sleep."
—*Rip Van Winkel*

The animals have gathered
in a circle around him, not sure
what to make of a man
so asleep in the woods—

asleep, they are certain,
because no buzzard circles,
no crow caws.
And no stench either, no

dogs from the town
for even man's best friend
can't resist
that primitive odor.

Yes, this sleep
defies all nature
and the animals have come
out of wonder:

the fox
and the rodent together
in awe of this slumber
deeper than the woodchuck's

in his infinite burrow,
the fat black bear's.
For twenty years
they will keep this vigil

and in the morning
when the man climbs back
into his body as after
a night's sleep

they will scatter
in the same old fear
who for once and once only
did not eat of his flesh, or one another's.

VULTURE

And once again
they too are back

high up each spring
on thermal drafts

above the green
to drift and tack

with tilting wings
like sails but black

because no songs
will fill their beaks

from picking clean
our mortal tracks

for what's to sing
of this one fact

their silence means,
this circling back?

THE CHOPPING BLOCK

In its center, a stain,
the dark core of maple—
a knot of dried blood,
a little twist of pain.

Here, the emperor laid his head,
loosened his linen collar.
Twiddling through centuries,
the chopped thumbs of thieves.

On this bull's eye
I put a log to split, heft
the bright blade, hear
the fat hen squawk.

In my darkest dreams I climb
the hill with my son. His curls
spill on the block. Knife raised,
I stare at the sky.

This block is so old
moss grows on its side.
Look into this compass, sailor.
Weep, for you are lost.

Bruce Guernsey

THE WATER WITCH

A curse and he's there,
dryness come for a drink
singing his song of thirst,
the wind like dust in his veins.

For a stick he takes
a snake from a sack,
holds the halves of its tongue,
walking your land for water.

At the spot where in your dreams
you shoveled a grave,
the tail quivers, drives downward
through the gnawed heart.

"Drink," he says, knowing your thirst,
the sweating cup in your hand.
In your throat it is cold and good,
with a taste of salt, like tears.

THE OWL

This morning, half way up
a snow-packed hill,
I spotted an owl
on a branch at the top.

Out of breath, I stopped,
watching it turn
at the crunch of my step.
In the cold, staring back,

the hangman's eyes,
the holes in his hood,
watching me climb,
coiling the slack.

THE SEEING-EYE DOG

sneaks out nights,
cool in beret,

his master's dark glasses,
sips cointreau

at the dog café
and watches;

is the poet of dogs
with a voice that sees

for the man who can't,
that speaks the meaning

of red, of green;
is the loneliest dog

at the dog café
where hounds down suds

and the barking
is loud.

Part Four

EISENSTAEDT'S KISS

I dream for my parents it was just like this:
the anonymous sailor, the anonymous nurse,

her head in his arm, his hand at her waist,
on Times-Square that day in August

about when my father came down the ramp
and they kissed like those strangers I hope,

bending together, my mother and father,
curve into curve, these mythical lovers.

TIMETABLE

Behind me this morning on the train,
in the early light made warm
through the window's double-glass,
an old Amish man,
the rough of his beard gone white,
is singing to his wife, both of them
round and red-faced as apples
in their simple clothes, bonnet and hat,
their seat on the Amtrak
one of those looking south
as we head north to Chicago.

My back against theirs,
I close my eyes to listen
but in the privacy of their language,
in the seclusion of their ways,
I can't make out the words
and hear instead the rails,
their heartbeat like hooves
as he hums to her in the sun,
one hand I dream in hers—the other, the reins,
their buggy's glass lamp swinging in time
toward their farm in Arthur.

Suddenly awake, suddenly alive,
feeling suddenly happier than I have in months,
I want to call them you and me,
to sing to you in words

some guy going to a meeting in the city
can't understand.
And oh, if I could hold your hand
just like that,
no one else on the train,
just the two of us in our buggy,
looking back.

LOOKING BACK

Looking back
through the kitchen window,
lit as always every night,
I see her by the sink, looking out,
so I wave and point
the way he might
at the steak I bought
on the grill,
their ritual meal
those Saturday nights
if my father made a sale—
she'd feed us first,
insist on prayers,
then off to bed
while downstairs
my father poured
two High Lifes in tall glasses
he'd hid all week for now,
then go outside
to light the charcoal—
I turn the gas down low,
look toward the light
and point again
to say the meat is almost done
but in the window
she can't see out
nor could she then
when she'd come down

to set the table
and he'd be busy where I am,
invisible, but there
in the dark, beer in hand,
and from that light
she'd wave to him.

THE SPECIALS

At eighty-five my grandfather,
blinking his way from Florida
to New Hampshire that spring, his last,
drove the by-pass around Atlanta
four or five full orbits, or so we figure,
before my grandmother, hungry again,
as fat as he was thin,
awoke beside him where she'd always ride
to ask if they could stop
for breakfast there this morning,
so good were the grits last May,
the coming summer come and gone
in the wink of her nap
and now we're heading back, she thought,
her sense of time like his of space
as he drifted toward an exit
through horns and middle-digits raised,
somehow finding north,
these two old ducks, though missing
the Stuckey's of her dreams
but finding, we're sure, another,
because they always stopped at this—
or was it that one?—for mid-day dinner,
side-by-side in their favorite booth
where for as long as anyone can remember
the same waitress brought
the sirloin special, chopped, for both.

FOR MY WIFE, CUTTING MY HAIR

You move around me expertly like the good, round
Italian barber I went to in Florence
years before we met, his scissors
a razor he sharpened on a belt.

But at first when you were learning, I feared
for my neck, saw my ears like sliced fruit
on the newspapered floor. Taking us back in time,
you cleverly clipped my head in a flat-top.

The years in between were styles no one had ever seen,
or should see again: when the wind rose
half my hair floated off in feathers,
the other half bristling, brief as a brush.

In the chair, almost asleep, I hear the bright
scissors dancing. Hear you hum, full-breasted as Aida,
carefully trimming the white from my temples,
so no one, not even I, will know.

GLOVE

If in this word
is love itself
then love is bone
and blood inside
the form that warms
your lovely hand—

your hand is love
and mine that takes
your love in mine
without your hand
is nothing but
an empty word.

CANOE

A swallow
skimming the pond at dusk,
how it tilts to the water
the curve of its wing.

I push off from shore,
casting for trout—
the dip of paddle, the silence,
nothing but ripples of breeze.

Imagine his hands,
the edge of his blade,
who hollowed this bird
from a log.

PASQUANEY

Night-fishing for bass,
I feed a line
over the stern
into the lake,
my long canoe slowly turning,
turning slowly
in the stillness,
the minnow I hooked in the lip
dragged by three beads of shot
beneath the drifting stars,
beyond the drop-off.

The drop-off—
how, as kids, it filled us with fear,
a shadowy line
marking the end
of the soft, safe sand
where our toes could touch—
that twilight ridge
where only the skilled adults
dared swim—

where later,
with goggles
and the diving push of fins,
I'd kick along the dreamlike slope
in search of mussels
to crack on stones for bait;

or, showing off my teenage arm,
would skip across the sunlit surface,
the flesh in those spinning shells,
a food, legend has it,
for the vanished Pasquaney.

A century ago,
long before the interstate,
before the condos and the lawnmower
buzz of outboards,
before, before, before,
the pines were stripped for pulp
and Lake Pasquaney claimed for power,
concrete and steel
pushing the water back.

Now, it's Newfound Lake,
miles longer, wider,
a beach where the woods
once were,
stumps smothered,
sand washing in, decades of sifting
and only a dark, watery line
to mark the passing.

The drop-off—
where light dims like memory
and the big fish hold
in ledges of granite,
in the cold oxygen—

where, on a brushy shore,
the French explorer
checked his traps,
salted hides, and paddled toward Canada—
where the last Pasquaney
once knelt to the water
and stared at the color of his skin.

Where an old road is,
I heard my grandfather say,
"the original road around the lake,
the real lake,
the road we used to ride"—
where wheels are rusting under me now,
big iron wheels
from the rattling carriage
bringing my grandparents north
the first time, my grandmother
in her Boston finery,
bustle and hat,
my grandfather offering his hand,
helping her down,
sunlight
glistening through the pines.

Starlight now,
a tap, tap on the line
as the minnow drops
deeper down into a sky
where fins fan the wheel ruts,

the ringing pressure in my ears,

holding my breath for one more mussel,

there, beyond the sand slowly

turning over the edge

into the stillness drowning

down, down, down,

into the crater of Lake Pasquaney.

EPITAPH

On top of a hill
one day in the fall

just up
from where I'd stopped

to try the well
by an old cellar hole,

I found, bleached as bone,
a headstone

blank without
the name or date—

no others at all
there on that knoll

retaken by alders
and saplings of poplar,

just that one, white
and mute,

cut by him
her dying left numb,

who'd shouldered it on
and cradled to ground

then closing his eyes
stood for a time

and touching that stone
turned back down.

Bruce Guernsey

THE VASE

May in March: our daughter's birthday, somehow now twenty
as the crocus uncurl in their black beds, everywhere
yellow, yellow, a whole week of weather
yellow as her hair—

even the bug light on the north porch
where a moth this birthday evening, back too soon,
flaps against the glass flower,
the dust of its wings on the yellow bloom.

In the mild of this scented night, so fragile,
we walk her to her car and back to college:
seat belt on, doors locked, half a carrot cake
in a box beside her and leaning against it the vase

we found and filled with twenty daffodils
to brighten the table tonight, yellow, yellow,
yellow as the petals from its delicate neck
like wishes we'd given light to, gone in a breath.

—for Amanda Littekin, 1975-1995

SOMETIMES FOR HOURS

At my feet my dog,
a pastoral scene,

master and beast,
except in his dream

he's chasing a car,
flinching awake

as the wheels hit—
the way we do

falling through sleep,
suddenly saved.

What the mind questions,
the heart believes

and we lie there reasoning,
afraid.

The dog instead
scratches his ear,

nips at a flea
and is soon back twitching.

But we,
we lie in the night

sometimes for hours
wondering

why the lights
that cross the ceiling

from a passing car
trouble us so,

a moment of light
in all that dark.

JANUARY THAW

This is the time of forgiveness,
when your father
would bend down to you
just before sleep,
the breath of his kiss
the warmth of this breeze
as you walk the slope
behind the house,
the land you'd forgotten
under the drifts:
how the stones,
steaming with light,
steady the earth
in the melting snow.

Bruce Guernsey

IMAGES OF WAR

Looking out the front window of my house
this spring morning, the soft rain greening
the new grass of late March
as civil wars rage daily on the TV screen,

I think of the greenhouses built from glass
once etched with the images of war:
barefoot men in muddy trenches dug
to hold back Grant at Petersburg,

the smoky negatives of their swollen bodies
sold by photographers gone broke
at the end of the war, glass plates
pieced together like cathedral windows

to heat the flats of roses underneath,
to green the new shoots, sunlight
thin at first, eclipsed by the dark of shoeless feet,
by the winter haze of empty hands

shading for a time the plants beneath,
then slowly like mist, like a rain cloud lifting,
slowly vanishing—an eye, the nose, his face—
the glass pure sky, a summer's day.

HOMAGE TO EDGAR BERGEN

I was a little kid
when the family would gather
and bow their heads
by the radio then

those Sunday nights
my grandfather inched
the glowing dial
from news of the war

to Charlie McCarthy
and Mortimer Snerd
to make us laugh
instead,

my Nana and aunts,
my mother, too,
in wonder at one voice
made into many—

and me, the son at home
they let stay up
to hear his special
kind of prayer,

the ventriloquist
who'd gone to bless
our men over there
with the miracle

of laughter, those boys
not made of wood
whose lips not even
he could move, after.

EXTRA INNINGS

The commemorative plaque on the trimmed lawn
of Indian Gap National Cemetery
has "Captain" inscribed before my father's name,
the highest rank among the honored around him,
the other soldiers missing, I presume, in action,
unlike my zany Pop who simply wandered off, AWOL
one spring from the Veteran's Hospital, his furlough,
    eternity.
He always marched to an off-beat drummer and then
    with Parkinson's
became a wind-up toy soldier who'd charge,
head down from the disease, straight on, elbowing
my mother's vases and crystal on his way
through enemy fire to the end of time.

Wherever he went that day, years ago now,
I see him leading a platoon
of men like those not there around him,
Purple Hearts and heroes, all of them, yes,
but not on this mission with a daffy Captain.
Instead, they've found their way to some green ballpark,
the 9000th inning about to start
and beer for all forever:
just a bunch of happy ghosts, waving to the camera.

THE LADY AND THE TRAMP

As my mother's memory dims
she's losing her sense of smell
and can't remember the toast
blackening the kitchen with smoke
or sniff how nasty the breath of the dog
that follows her yet from room to room,
unable, himself, to hear his own bark.

It's thus they get around,
the wheezing old hound stone deaf
baying like a smoke alarm
for his amnesiac mistress whose back
from petting him is bent forever
as they shuffle toward the flaming toaster
and split the cindered crisp that's left.

THE PRESENT

For her birthday this year
I bought my mother
one of those portable phones,
the kind you can carry
all over the house
so she won't be alone
anywhere anymore,

except she can't remember
where she's left it
most of the time these days
and hurries in her slippers
from one room to the next
only to hear it ringing
somewhere down the hall

and opens the front door
to no one there
or still on the phone
when she finally finds it
where she never put it,
the house getting bigger
as she gets smaller

but no less busy
than she was before
with us six kids
and my father at work, or war—
this new phone like having us
still around, calling from somewhere,
upstairs or down.

THE PASSING

I dream today,
because it is snowing,
of my father's bones
under the snow,
of the passing of seasons
wherever he lay down
that last time
in the late May woods,
his flesh now
long since
carried away, no odor
on the wind anymore,
just the scrubbed white
of those bones,
another year
of spring rain,
honeysuckle like twine
and bright leaves
falling, blowing,
and now again the snow—
this time of year
the deer together
under the evergreens,
seed swelling
in the shy does,
the bucks grown meek
whose antlers once thrashed
the pine branches,
whose antlers will soon
be no more than bones,
whitening, under the snow,
under the deepening snow.

FROM RAIN

Around Easter
when the woods are still pastel
and the air is damp with April,
I need to feel the river's pull
I haven't felt all winter,

this longing I have for water
that leads me here where cutbanks swell
with spring from every hill,
mysterious, maternal,
and into that fullness I enter,

myself no longer
but one with the shifting gravel,
and, like these mayflies hatching in swirls,
from rain I've come, will spinning fall
as once and ever,

both son and father,
eternal and ephemeral
while the current around me curls
and I lift my line in this ritual
of rod and river, of Adam and lover.

-- for Victoria

Author's Note

From Rain: Poems 1970-2010 is a collection gleaned from four books and seven chapbooks, as well as from new and previously uncollected poetry. The poems are arranged thematically, not chronologically, to make a more unified book.

Forty years of writing poems means that I have had a lot of encouragement along the way, but long before I ever wrote a word, I learned so much about poetry from Professor Bruce Berlind when I was an undergraduate at Colgate University. His precise reading of a poem led me to strive for precision in writing one.

I would like to thank all of those who read my early work and cheered me on, some especially, like Dave Smith, who published my first chapbook with his Back Door Press in 1970, and the late William Matthews with his remarkable critical eye.

How lucky I have been over these years to have had such special poetry friends like Donald Hall, Charles Simic, and Robert Fagles. I can't thank Ted Kooser enough for including four of the poems here in his weekly column *American Life in Poetry.* And you, Joe Kennedy, better known as "X.J.," you generous man, how kind you've been using two of these poems in later editions of your iconic text, *An Introduction to Poetry,* ironically the first book I used as a beginning instructor in 1967.

No doubt I have tried the patience of even the best of friends like Ken Green at William and Mary and Andy Orr at Virginia Wesleyan, who read my fledgling attempts with remarkable generosity. As a teacher, I have had the privilege of learning, and I want to thank both Denise Preston and Elise Hempel, former students and fine poets themselves, for their reading so many early drafts during my years at Eastern Illinois University and now.

These poems and I have also had the generous help of residency fellowships at the MacDowell Colony, the Ragdale Foundation, and Hawthornden Castle in Scotland, plus grants and awards from the NEA, the Illinois Arts Council, and the Fulbright Commission.

My children have been my muse, and their mother a model of hard work and intelligence. There are no words I can write here to thank them. These poems will have to do.

Meanwhile, working at her jewelry bench each day, crafting bits of the earth into pattern and color, there is my wife Victoria, the real shaper of symbols. The ring she made for my finger is proof.

CPSIA information can be obtained at www.ICGtesting.com
Printed in the USA
BVOW041858280212

283953BV00001B/2/P